How to use these notes

Guided Rea[...]

GW01464197

Walkthrough/[...] [...]-3)

A *walkthrough*, or book introd[...] [...]oup of children. During the walkthro[...] [...]s and significant vocabulary they will meet when they read the book.

Go through the whole of the walkthrough before the children start reading independently. The walkthrough notes on pages 2 and 3 of this booklet provide prompts for you to use, specific to *Boring Old Bed*. The questions, comments and suggestions alert children to ideas and vocabulary they will need in order to read independently and with full understanding.

Independent Reading (pages 4–5)

After the walkthrough, ask the children to read the text aloud, on their own, at their own pace. Observe the strategies each child uses, praising successful problem solving and expressive reading. Prompts are suggested for good phrasing, use of word-solving skills, predicting and checking the meaning, and actively monitoring the implications of the text, on pages 4 and 5.

After Independent Reading/ Returning to the text (page 6)

After the children have read the book independently, return to the text as a group to reinforce teaching points and to check children's understanding. On page 6, there are quick follow-up ideas for related text, sentence and word level work.

Responding to the text (pages 6–8)

It is important to encourage children to give a personal response to the text. Discussion ideas related to the book are on page 6.

These Teaching Notes also contain group activity ideas on page 7, and a Photocopy Master on page 8, for use after the guided reading session or in a follow-up literacy session.

Guided Reading Notes

Ask the children to read the title and back cover blurb and to predict what the story is about.

Pages 2–3

PROMPTS What is happening in the pictures? Ask the children to find the main characters in the story *(Charlie, mum, dad, granny, little brother, dog)*.

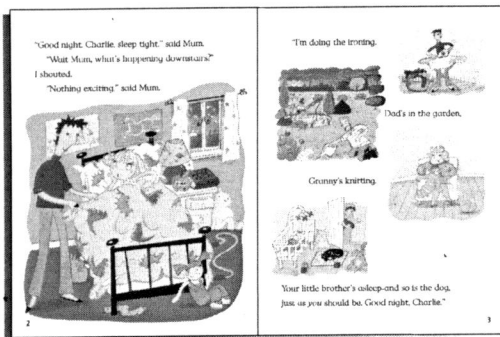

Pages 4–5

PROMPTS Charlie is in bed upstairs, and she's bored. (Read the refrain to the children, and explain that she's telling the story.) The picture on page 5 shows us what Charlie is imagining her mum is doing downstairs.

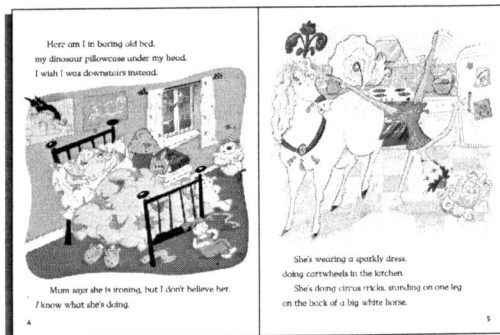

Pages 6–7

PROMPTS What's Charlie doing in this picture? (Prompt for *she's in bed*. Draw children's attention to the rhyming words at the end of the lines on page 6 – *bed, head, instead*. Read the lines together, using expression and pace appropriate to the rhythm and rhyme.)

This time she's imagining what her dad is doing. Let's look at the picture to see what she thinks he's doing. (Introduce the phrase *scuba diving* – using a breathing device underwater.) What else can you see in the picture? (Prompt for *octopus* and *mermaid*. Have the children spotted the angling gnome, on the pond's surface?)

But here am I in boring old bed,
my dinosaur pillowcase under my head.
I wish I was downstairs instead.

I don't think Dad is watering the plants
or mowing the lawn.

6

Dad's scuba diving in the garden.
First he's wrestling with a big octopus,
next he's rescuing a beautiful silvery mermaid.

7

Now ask the children to look quickly through pages 8 to 14 and comment on what Charlie imagines is happening.

Pages 14–15

PROMPTS Charlie's gone downstairs to check what everyone's doing. What do you think she will see?

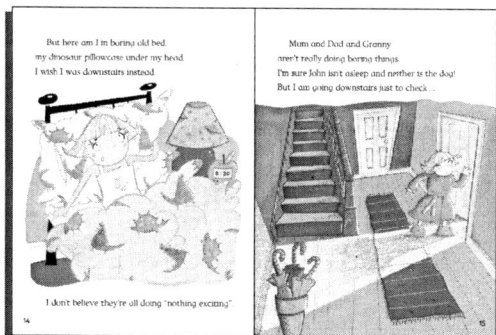

But here am I in boring old bed,
my dinosaur pillowcase under my head.
I wish I was downstairs instead.

I don't believe they're all doing "nothing exciting".

14

Mum and Dad and Granny
aren't really doing boring things.
I'm sure John isn't asleep and neither is the dog!
But I am going downstairs just to check ...

15

Tell the children not to turn to page 16, but go back to the start of the story and start reading independently.

Before the children start reading, talk for a moment about the pace and expression appropriate to the rhythm and rhyme of Charlie's refrain.

Pages 2–3

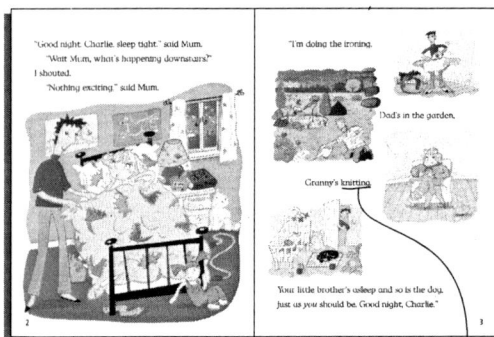

knitting
"The 'k' is silent in this word. Look at the illustration to double-check."

CHECK for accurate reading of *exciting*.

"The c sounds like s in this word. Look for known letter clusters *(ex, ing)* and blend through the word. Read on and check that your attempt makes sense."

Pages 4–5

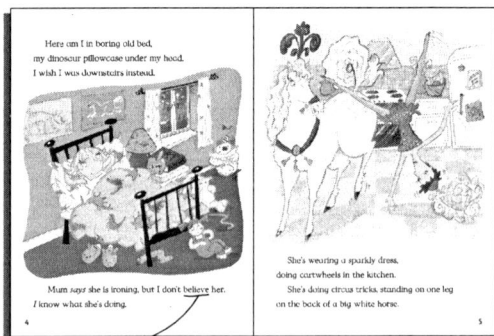

believe
"Leave a gap and read on. Then reread from the start of the sentence and think about what would make sense."

CHECK that the child can split *downstairs* and *cartwheels* into their component parts.

"Look for a word that you know. Try covering up the end of the word before you read it."

CHECK for expressive reading, especially of words in italics.

"Who's telling the story? Can you make it sound as if Charlie's talking?"

**beautiful
silvery**
"Split the word into syllables. Look for known letter clusters and blend through the word."

CHECK that the child uses picture clues to support reading.

"Can you find Dad in the picture? What's he doing? What else can you see?"

Ask the child to read on, checking that he or she reads with plenty of expression.

Pages 14–15

CHECK that the child reads the contracted words *aren't* and *isn't* accurately, and is aware of the grammatical agreement.

"The apostrophe shows that some letters are missing. Think about what would make sense. What does the apostrophe replace?"

Page 16

CHECK Were you right – what did Charlie see?
Do you think this is a 'real' picture?

After Independent Reading/Returning to the text

Word knowledge – secure the short vowel phoneme *ea* (head)

Write the words *head* and *instead* on the flipchart. Ask children to identify the letters that make the *e* sound in these words. Ask children to suggest other words with the same spelling for the vowel phoneme *ea*. If necessary, suggest a word by asking riddles about the target words, such as: *you can eat this with butter*. Examples include *bread, dread, lead, read, spread*, and *measure*.

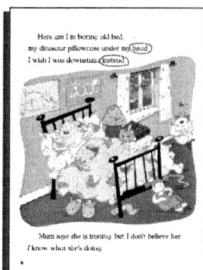

Sentence knowledge – read aloud with pace and expression

Read pages 10 and 11 again, this time concentrating on reading with pace and expression. Discuss the way the rhyme and the repetition reinforce the way nothing changes upstairs, whatever happens elsewhere.

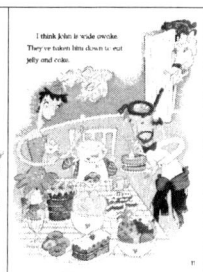

Text knowledge – respond imaginatively to humorous stories

Look at the picture. Ask the children to comment on whether they think Charlie is imagining this scene. Do they think the illustrations add to the humour? How? Can the children dream up some exciting things that their own families might like to do?

Responding to the text

- Ask the children why they think Charlie is unable to sleep.
- What does Charlie think is happening downstairs?
- Ask the children what they think is really happening.
- What kind of girl do they think Charlie is?

1 Counting syllables

AIM to discriminate syllables in multi-syllabic words (*NLS: Y2 T2 W5*)

YOU WILL NEED
● small cards with multi-syllabic words from the text written onto them, e.g. *dinosaur, pillowcase, watering, octopus, beautiful, silvery, mermaid, motorbike, dragon*
● scissors

WHAT TO DO Ask children to identify how many syllables there are in the words above by clapping to them as they say the word out loud. Clap the syllables to phrases such as *dinosaur pillowcase, watering the plants, beautiful, silvery mermaid, big red motorbike*.

Clap children's names and ask them to identify their own name from the number of syllables clapped.

Using the cards with multi-syllabic words from the text, demonstrate where the syllable breaks are by cutting the words into syllables. Place the cards on the table and play a game in which children grab 2 or 3 cards and try to make a word from the syllables. Discuss the words made – are they real?

2 Bedtime stories

AIM to use story structure to write about own experience
(*NLS: Y2 T1 T6, T10*)

YOU WILL NEED ● flip chart

WHAT TO DO Discuss with the children what they think their parents or other family members do after the children have gone to bed, e.g. household chores, gardening, watch television, listen to music, or other hobbies. Now ask the children to imagine exciting alternatives to these activities. Explain that they are going to use the structure of *Boring Old Bed* to write about their own family. You may wish to write a sentence starter on the flipchart, e.g.
When I am tucked up in bed, I don't believe Mum is …
I know what she's doing. She's …

Make a poster

HAVE YOU SEEN THIS PERSON?

Name: _____

Age: _____

Description: _____

_____

Secret hobbies: _____

_____

Ask children to make a wanted poster using the frame above. They can write about a character from the book, or someone from their own family. Remind them of the secret hobbies the characters had in the book, and encourage them to invent something equally imaginative for their own character.

Boring Old Bed   *(NLS: Y2 T2 T14; S9)*